"LEEDS UPON AIRE"

The tiny hamlet of "Loidis in Elmete" was founded on the north bank of the River Aire well over a thousand years ago, probably on the line of the Roman Road between Chester and York. Its geographical location was ideal, with its hinterland rich in produce such as wool, skins, grain and root crops.

The cloth trade made Leeds one of England's most important towns and with this strong economic base it was to become one of the great "boom" towns of the Industrial Revolution. This came about not only because of its central location in northern England but because of a series of developments in the transport field that were to make Leeds a very accessible place. In a traffic and transport sense, "its all been happening" around here for two centuries.

In 1770 work commenced on the Leeds and Liverpool Canal linking it with the River Aire (it was not until 1816 that it was completed). However, it was not long before the age of steam locomotives arrived in mid-century and high viaducts were built running into the four railway stations shown on the 1847 Ordnance survey map (only one of which survives today as part of the present Leeds City Station).

To bring the story up-to-date, the M1 Motorway discharges into the city only a few hundred yards from Leeds Bridge. This walk will take you through and around an incredible network of water, locks, viaducts, bridges and tracks all within a very compact area. Not to forget some interesting, unusual and sometimes bizarre buildings and structures which are to be found in this corner of the city.

All this activity has created problems in that Leeds has tended to "turn its back" on the River Aire and the Canal. The main railway route through the city centre runs east-west just north of the waterways and its high viaduct forms a strong physical and visual barrier between the bustling shopping streets and the Waterfront. However, years of neglect and dereliction in the lands south of the viaduct are being swept away and the waterside is being opened up for the enjoyment of citizens and visitors.

Leeds Civic Trust has campaigned for waterfront regeneration since its founding in 1965, to "put Leeds-upon-Aire". Several guides on waterfront walks have been published by the Trust, this being the most recent. However, it was not until the 1980s that confidence and, consequently investment, enabled developments to proceed. Major projects such as Victoria Quays, The Chandlers and the Design Innovation Centre were realised east of Leeds Bridge (see our guide "Leeds Waterfront East"). West of the bridge the ASDA offices and the Embankment were planned or built and Granary Wharf was functioning.

This waterside renaissance continued after the inception in 1988 of the Leeds Development Corporation (LDC), one of several sponsored by the Government to regenerate inner-city areas. The LDC became the planning authority for much of south and central Leeds and the Kirkstall Valley, providing much needed investment for overall environmental and infrastructure improvements as well as grant assistance for individual projects.

Neglect and decay is giving way to attractive environments where the old industrial character is being conserved and carefully blended with new uses including commercial, residential and leisure activities. Life has returned to the waterfront and though the old cranes are idle now you can still find traces of former industrial activity side by side with the craft shows, festival markets and colourful narrow-boats.

The Trust is committed to a policy that calls for the rejuvenation of the Leeds Waterways by a careful balance of conservation and new developments that will foster the return of a working and residential community, the cleaning of the river and encouragement for those who would use it for recreational and commercial purposes.

After all, why should the city not bear the title "Leeds-Upon-Aire"?

THE WALK

1 This bridge was built in 1873, replacing an original medieval structure which was the site of the famous Leeds Cloth Market in the 17th century. The bridge was the only crossing point between Kirkstall and Swillington until the early 19th century, and so was very important.

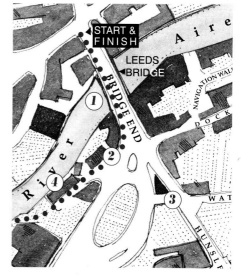

From the bridge can be viewed from left to right: the unusual bridgehead building with its prominent clock, the four-storey warehouse at 2 Water Lane, now nicely restored, and the *ASDA head offices* (described below). Across the river (on the north side) the site of new commercial developments at Sovereign Quays and, on the right bridgehead, Windsor House, a recently converted building.

It is intended that *a new road bridge* will be constructed just upstream of Leeds Bridge, passing by the end of ASDA. Though some minor diversions may be necessary during construction, full waterside access for pedestrians is promised on completion.

Proceed south, to your left, turn to your right and pause outside the Old Red Lion.

2 This is an attractive public house of early 19th century origin, and is said to be the oldest pub left in the city centre. Note the fine lion statue above the entrance. The exterior has been nicely restored in recent years. Note also the leaded-light windows.

3 Across the road to the left of the Red Lion, note the tall red brick building, *Leeds Bridge House*. This was built as a Temperance hotel about 1875, but later housed a variety of functions. Very unusual in its form, brought about by its restricted site, this structure has been compared with New York's Flat-Iron building which it preceded by over 20 years. The contrasting "layers" of arches display some remarkable craftsmanship in brick.

Proceed along Water Lane to the right of the Red Lion. Pause outside No 2 Water Lane.

4 This *beautifully proportioned early 19th century warehouse* building is now in office use having been carefully restored in recent years.

Carry on along Water Lane eventually entering the new riverside path, and pause when you reach the lowered jetty area.

5 To your left *the large ASDA office HQ* completed in 1988. This occupies a long riverside frontage and, as part of the scheme, an *attractive landscaped walkway* was provided for the public. The use of this site was an important catalyst in the redevelopment of what had become a derelict eyesore along the waterfront, and others were to follow. This fine new building occupies the site of

the first Leeds Quaker Meeting House and burial ground (1699). When you reach the west end of the block you can see a plaque recording this fact.

Across the river to your right the new Sovereign Quays development (and possibly the new river bridge).

6 To its left, *Victoria Mills* (begun in 1836 and restored 1992) is a bold group of brick buildings grouped around an attractive landscaped courtyard that opens up to the riverside. Over the years these old buildings seemed to have housed a bewildering variety of users. Note the new projecting river walk structure that takes you around the *Leodis Restaurant.* The top of the gable should be noted with its datestone.

Proceed a little further on the walkway, pause at the end of the ASDA block.

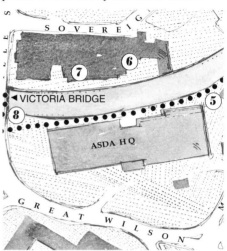

7 Across the river to the right of Victoria Bridge is the *Embankment,* a group of new office buildings whose architectural form is varied and articulated by contrast with the ASDA approach opposite. They are in contrasting brick and an interesting riverside walk has been provided that leads from a spacious paved terrace by the bridge under and through the various buildings.

8 To the immediate left of the Embankment is *Victoria Bridge.* Perhaps *the most handsome bridge in the city,* it was completed in 1839 and named after the young Queen who had been crowned only two years prior. The simple arch has huge stones which were quarried locally and the Queen's name is celebrated on the central parapet. The stone bridge replaced a timber footbridge of 1829 but lost in a flood in 1837.

Proceed up the riverside walkway to Neville Street. Cross the road via the central refuge, taking very great care (this is where the M1 discharges into central Leeds). Turn right and pause at the centre of Victoria Bridge.

9 From here there is a good panorama of *the Canal Basin, a major feature of our walk, and this is where the "transport network" in our Introduction is entered.* From the bridge can be viewed (left to right): the new offices of the *Medical Protection Society (1994)* in front of which the *Hol Beck* enters the river from a culvert, the *Canal Warehouse and River Lock,* the open Canal Basin with its graving docks, *the railway viaduct and Leeds City Station* in the background, *the River Aire flowing through huge brick arches* and the tall Hilton International Hotel. (All these features described later.) Immediately below you and to your right, *the former coal staithes* and wharf for the city. Latterly, this was taken over by the Co-op who used two rail-mounted steam cranes to unload barges. One of the cranes remains, the other is preserved at Armley Mills Museum.

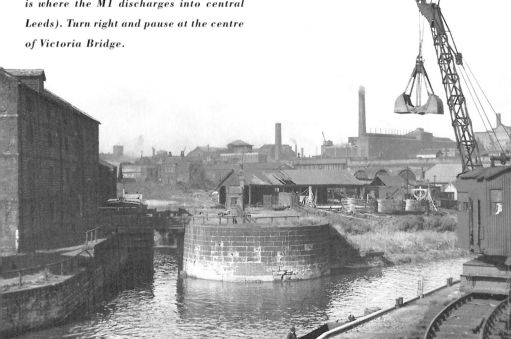

The atmosphere is marvellous on the bridge, particularly when the Aire is in spate and the river thunders through the narrow arches. Looking upstream, a medieval dam still exists, originally diverting water into goits that discharged back into the river by Leeds Bridge. These goits provided the power for the Manorial Corn Mills. *One of the most dramatic and bizarre places in the city, the Dark Arches have been compared with the settings from the Lord of the Rings and those by Piranesi.*

Proceed north along Neville Street, pause outside the Hilton International Hotel.

10 This was opened in 1973 and its height and mass is increased by the virtue of having parking at lower levels. Recently a glazed atrium extension has been added. As will be seen later, *the Hilton visually dominates the Canal Basin* and its surroundings.

Walk further up Neville Street going under the railway bridge, turning left at the sign for "Granary Wharf". Go along the tunnel and pause on the iron bridge over the River Aire.

11 You are now under the *"Dark Arches"*, the local name for the huge tunnels and vaults that lie beneath the railway viaduct and the City Station. The progressive expansion of the railways over the years has created *an incredible network of magnificent brick arches, a civil engineering marvel.*

Carry on along the tunnel passing by the various shops set under the arches. At the end, turn right into the Granary Wharf Craft Arcade.

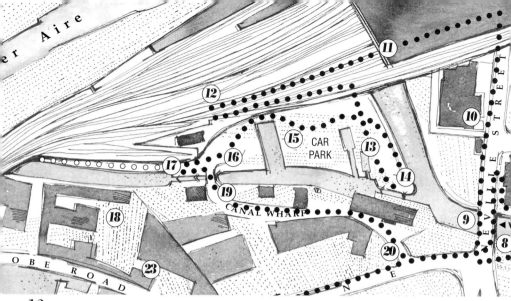

12 *In the 1980s the Dark Arches were gradually transformed into a significant visitor attraction.* This area is furnished with period-style shop units set within attractively floodlit vaults. At weekends and holidays the Craft Arcade is supplemented by a few dozen temporary stalls that are set within the arches. *Jugglers, fire eaters, musicians and others entertain visitors at weekends,* adding colour to the bustling scene.

Leave the Craft Arcade, return a little way along the tunnel and go right out onto the open land outside the viaduct. Proceed through the car park towards the large warehouse to your left. Pause at the graving docks.

13 These *dry docks* were used for building and maintaining boats. The larger one provides both wet and dry docks and was built about 1790. *Boatyards existed here into this century* and it was also the main slate and stone wharfage for Leeds.

Proceed to the River Lock and Canal Warehouse.

14   The first lock on the Leeds and Liverpool Canal has a lift of over 11 feet from river to basin. The great curve of the stone retaining wall beside the lock is typical of the civil engineering works of that period, strong and uncompromising (rather like the Dark Arches).

The lock is integral with the *Leeds and Liverpool Canal Warehouse*, across the canal. A massive building (1777), it was used for housing goods which could originally be loaded and off-loaded under cover from an internal canal branch which entered the building at the right-hand end. *The walls of the building increase in thickness towards the ground, giving an impression of great strength.* This is further stressed by the tiny windows set within substantial stone walls. The building was a granary late last century. Today it is proposed for use as offices with a restaurant at ground floor.

Return to the viaduct where you left the Craft Arcade. Walk alongside the viaduct, pausing by the old crane to your left.

15   This is *one of three remaining cranes* in the Canal Basin, and is to be retained as an historic feature. This canal branch formerly ran under the viaduct (note: bricked-up arches) linking with the Aire. This enabled coal boats to serve the former Leeds Power Station which stood on Whitehall Road (but recently demolished)

Walk from the crane to the Canal Bridge.

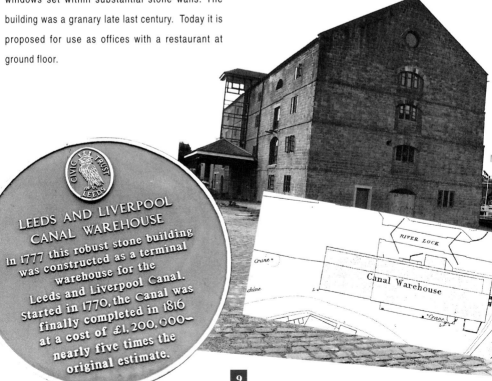

LEEDS AND LIVERPOOL CANAL WAREHOUSE
In 1777 this robust stone building was constructed as a terminal warehouse for the Leeds and Liverpool Canal. Started in 1770, the Canal was finally completed in 1816 at a cost of £1,200,000 — nearly five times the original estimate.

16 This attractive little stone structure is the first (or the last!) canal overbridge. It was built in 1841 replacing the original of the 1770s. *It is decorated with panels whose shape might well indicate influences emanating from the cast-iron bridges of the Grand Union Canal in the Midlands!*

This area has *moorings for pleasure craft* and is also the base for a trip boat which offers short trips at weekends or for group-hire. Restaurant facilities on the boat are available and *trips can proceed west up the canal or east downstream along the Aire.*

British Waterways

Office Lock

Walk up the steps to the right of the bridge
and proceed forward along the towpath
pausing at the lock.

17 This is known as *Office Lock*, since the
original Canal Office lies across the canal, just
behind the lock-keeper's house.

LEEDS AND LIVERPOOL CANAL

MOTOR CAR ACTS 1896 AND 1903

NOTICE

THIS **BRIDGE** IS **INSUFFICIENT**
TO CARRY A **HEAVY MOTOR CAR**, THE
REGISTERED AXLE-WEIGHTS OF ANY AXLE OF WHICH
EXCEEDS **THREE TONS** OR THE REGISTERED
AXLE-WEIGHTS OF THE SEVERAL AXLES OF WHICH
EXCEED IN THE AGGREGATE **FIVE TONS** OR A
HEAVY MOTOR CAR DRAWING A **TRAILER**,
IF THE REGISTERED AXLE-WEIGHTS OF THE SEVERAL
AXLES OF THE **HEAVY MOTOR CAR** AND THE AXLE-
WEIGHTS OF THE SEVERAL AXLES OF THE **TRAILER**
EXCEED IN THE AGGREGATE **FIVE TONS.**
PALL MALL,   BY ORDER,
LIVERPOOL. LEEDS & LIVERPOOL CANAL COMPANY.

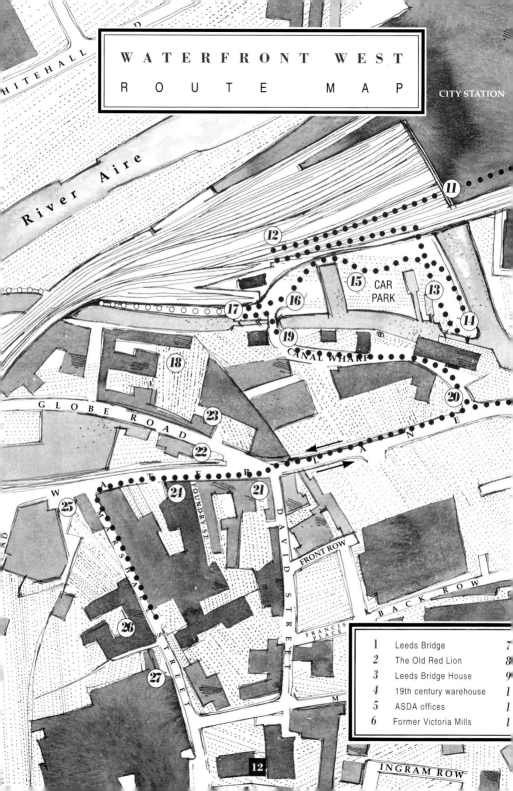

WATERFRONT WEST
ROUTE MAP

CITY STATION

River Aire

11
12
15 CAR PARK
13
16
17 14
19
CANAL WHARF
18
20
GLOBE ROAD
23
22
25 24 21
W A T E R . . . L A N E
26 FOUNDRY ST
DAVID STREET
27 FRONT ROW
BACK ROW
FRANCIS PLACE
WHITEHALL
MARSHALL STREET
INGRAM ROW

1	Leeds Bridge	7
2	The Old Red Lion	8
3	Leeds Bridge House	9
4	19th century warehouse	1
5	ASDA offices	1
6	Former Victoria Mills	1

12

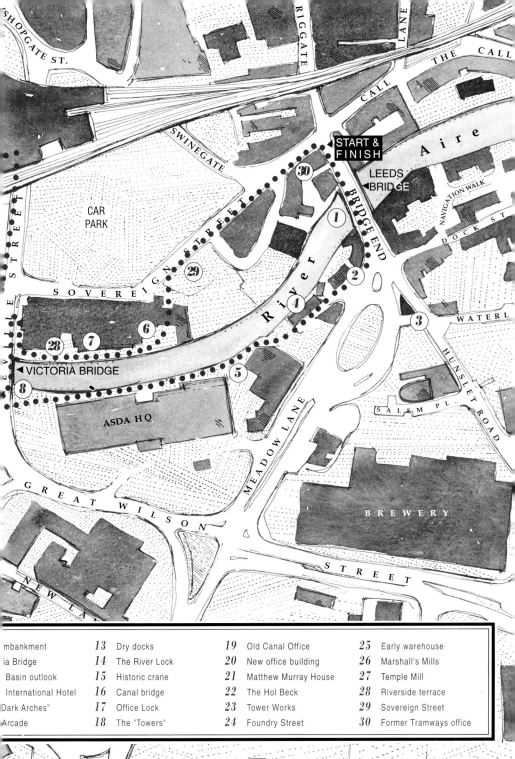

mbankment		**13** Dry docks	**19** Old Canal Office	**25** Early warehouse
ia Bridge		**14** The River Lock	**20** New office building	**26** Marshall's Mills
Basin outlook		**15** Historic crane	**21** Matthew Murray House	**27** Temple Mill
International Hotel		**16** Canal bridge	**22** The Hol Beck	**28** Riverside terrace
Dark Arches"		**17** Office Lock	**23** Tower Works	**29** Sovereign Street
Arcade		**18** The "Towers"	**24** Foundry Street	**30** Former Tramways office

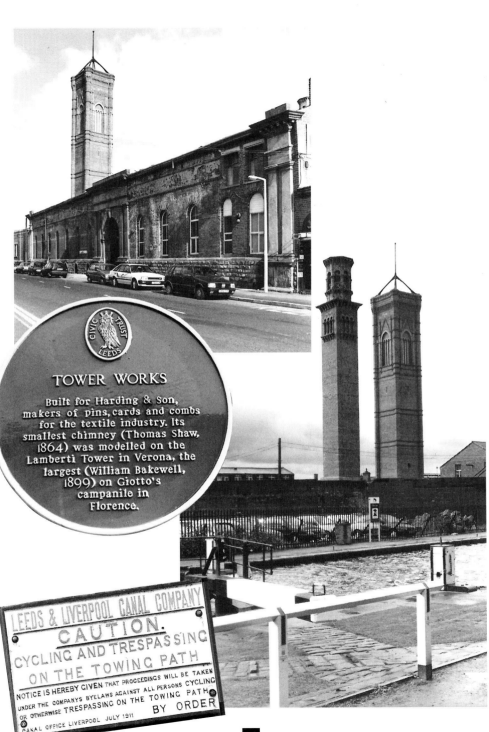

CIVIC TRUST LEEDS

TOWER WORKS

Built for Harding & Son, makers of pins, cards and combs for the textile industry. Its smallest chimney (Thomas Shaw, 1864) was modelled on the Lamberti Tower in Verona, the largest (William Bakewell, 1899) on Giotto's campanile in Florence.

LEEDS & LIVERPOOL CANAL COMPANY
CAUTION.
CYCLING AND TRESPASSING ON THE TOWING PATH

NOTICE IS HEREBY GIVEN THAT PROCEEDINGS WILL BE TAKEN UNDER THE COMPANYS BYELAWS AGAINST ALL PERSONS CYCLING OR OTHERWISE TRESPASSING ON THE TOWING PATH

BY ORDER

CANAL OFFICE LIVERPOOL JULY 1911

18 From here can be viewed some further features of an unusual nature, *the "Towers"*. Situated at Tower Works, Globe Road, Holbeck (which made needles and steel pins) are two brick Italian-style campaniles. The larger one known as the Giotto Tower is modelled on a tower at the cathedral in Florence (1334) and was built in 1899, functioning as an extract ventilation shaft. The other, smaller tower is a chimney which was built in 1864, replicating a 12th century Lamberti tower in Verona. *Victorian architects often dressed up their buildings in imported architectural styles and Leeds is very rich in examples. This appealed to the taste of the new wealthy business class, in this case the owner, Col. Harding, then Lord Mayor and creator of City Square.*

At this point, and if you have more time to spare, *you might like a walk along the towpath?*

A Side Trip (described later on page 24) will enable you to see the city from some unusual angles and you can make it as long or short a walk as you wish. *To resume the principal route, return, turning right onto the canal bridge. Pause at the Canal Office.*

19 *The old Canal Office and Lock-Keepers house* originally administered waterways' affairs but is no longer used as such. Across from the Office there is a good view of the Canal Basin. The Basin, the Leeds and Liverpool Canal terminus, changed radically when the railway arrived in 1846 and has seen many changes for the worse ever since. There is now a feeling of optimism that the demise has been arrested and that better things are on the horizon. *The view from the bridge is impressive* with the high buildings in the city centre forming a contrasting backdrop.

Leave the bridge, bearing left into Canal Wharf. Proceed to the junction with Water Lane. Pause to view two buildings.

20 There are *strong contrasts* between the old warehouse (already visited and described at 14 above) and the new national offices of the Medical Protection Society (1994). The former was built in the industrial functional tradition, an honest engineering solution as seen in its robust structure. The new offices are more consciously "designed" to meet a demanding brief calling for 20th century high technology working space, but enclosed with well-crafted Queen Anne-style facades.

At this point our walk leaves the waterfront so that historic Hol beck can be visited. Proceed from point 20, west along Water Lane, keeping to the right-hand side by the Hol Beck in its culvert. Pause at the junction with Globe Road.

Hol beck was the birthplace of Leeds factory industry in the 18th and 19th centuries, with such famous names as John Marshall and Matthew Murray having founded their factories here. The area cannot be described as beautiful today, being somewhat run-down and unsightly. But there is much of interest to be discovered.

21 Across the road, *Matthew Murray House*, at the junction with David Street. Though the present building is relatively new, it stands on the site of the Round Foundry where Murray, a young engineer *"who walked to Leeds in 1787 in search of work"* from Stockton-on-Tees, set up his own works in 1795. He had worked for John Marshall at Scotland Mill, Adel, in the Meanwood Valley, and was to continue this relationship later in Hol beck. *Murray is perhaps more famous for his railway engineering*, in 1812 designing locomotives for the Middleton Railway, reputedly the first commercial route in the world. Next, view Hol Beck and Tower Works.

22 *The Hol Beck* runs in culvert alongside Water Lane. Prior to the Industrial Revolution it was described as a "pleasant stream meandering through green meadows." Its waters were even bottled, being thought to possess medicinal properties!

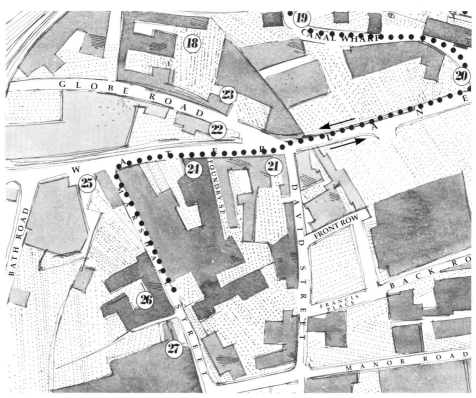

23 Just along Globe Road can be seen the impressive facade and monumental gateway of *Tower Works* (Civic Trust plaque), above which rise the Italian-style towers described at 18 on page 15.

Cross over Water Lane, pausing to view the Matthew Murray plaque, then turn right along Water Lane. Pause at the junction with Foundry Street.

24 Foundry Street was part of Murray's Round Foundry of c.1800 and the rows of old industrial buildings lining both sides of this street are now listed.

Proceed further along Water Lane pausing at the landscaped corner with Marshall Street.

John Marshall (1765-1845) gave his name to this street and 3 significant buildings (all listed) remain between Water Lane and Manor Road, evidence of his importance as an early Leeds industrialist. Son of a Briggate draper, he started spinning flax in Adel in 1787, using water power. It was then that *he met Matthew Murray to begin a very successful partnership,* moving to Holbeck in 1806, adopting steam power. Over 50 years or so, Marshall became very rich. However, though a stern employer, he was paternalistic, providing a school, baths and medical care for his workers.

25 The first building, in front of you, was built late in the 18th century as a warehouse and mechanics' shops. The other side of the block is more interesting, perhaps.

Walk along Marshall Street pausing in front of the tall buildings to your right.

26 *This block comprises three mills built in 1817, 1826 and 1830, forming an "E" shape on plan.* Five and six storey buildings are uncommon for this period and there are interesting iron roof-structures (not accessible to the public). However, another feature can be seen, *the inverted brick arches at street level* were a structural device that spread out the heavy loads from the brick pillars more evenly onto the foundations.

Walk further along Marshall Street and pause at the front of Temple Mill.

27 *You are looking at perhaps the most remarkable building in Leeds.* It was the final mill built by John Marshall and two sons at the height of their flax spinning business. *Listed Grade I as being of national architectural significance*, it is in two distinct parts with the mill (1838-40) to the left of the offices (1843). The factory is a single storey building covering two acres, lit by 65 conical roof lights. As such it pre-dates the many modern factories planned on one level by many years. Technically, the flax spinning process called for strict temperature and humidity control and forced air heating and evaporation channels were included. The flat roof was well insulated, being topped off with turf. *There is evidence that sheep were grazed on the roof!*

TEMPLE MILL

The magnificent but highly functional flax spinning mill to your left was erected by John Marshall, founder of the Leeds Flax Industry. Joseph Bonomi modelled it and this office building (added in 1843) on the Egyptian temple at Edfu.

Erected 1838-40

The office block is more decorative than the mill with a central entrance between groups of three papyrus headed capitals and set back glazing. It has decorative mouldings derived from Edfu, Egypt. This type of Egyptian decoration on Victorian buildings is thought to be unique on an

industrial building, the style usually being found on tombs and in cemeteries. *The architect, Joseph Bonomi, spent ten years in Egypt studying temples and pyramids.* The Leeds Civic Trust plaque recognises the importance of these buildings.

John Marshall died in 1845 and from then the flax business declined until closure in 1886. Since then the mills have housed a variety of users, latterly Kay's Mail Order Company.

Return to point 20 by taking the outwards route in reverse. To resume the principal route walk to the junction with Neville Street crossing over via the central refuge, taking very great care. Turn left, cross the bridge then immediately turn right passing through the gate and down the steps onto the riverside terrace.

28 *Time for a rest!* This attractive space is well sheltered and provided with seats, just the sort of place that is needed every so long beside the waterfront. There are good views of Victoria Bridge and ASDA, across the river.

Leave the terrace, proceeding along the walkway and passing through or alongside the new office buildings. Turn left when you reach the small gardens enclosed by the Victoria Mills. Pass through these and under the archway, emerging in Sovereign Street.

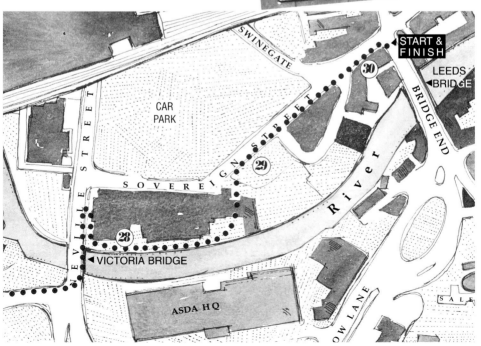

Walk along Sovereign Street, pausing at its junction with Swinegate.

30 On your right *the impressive offices of the former Leeds City Tramways* with the high ornamental archway above the stairs. Built in 1903, this was the HQ of the huge city department that gave way to Yorkshire Rider on de-regulation. *Proceed forward and when you reach Briggate turn right and back onto Leeds Bridge.*

You are now back where you commenced the walk. We hope you have found it interesting and enjoyable. *Why not get a copy of our other guided tour booklet "Leeds Waterfront East" and see more of our re-vitalised city?*

29 *This area has seen substantial changes over the centuries* and is still in the process of redevelopment. In 18th and 19th century maps several goits or water channels are seen to cross, discharging into the Aire west of Leeds Bridge. *John Cossins' map (1725)* shows Low Tenter, tenters being the frames used by cloth makers to stretch their materials by the riverbank in the 17th and 18th centuries. *The Leeds woollen industry was born in this area some 400 years ago.*

An extract of the 1847 Ordnance Survey map showing the area between Victoria and Leeds Bridges. Note the large mill goit (now filled) and the absence of the railway viaduct which now cuts across Swinegate and Neville Street.

SIDE TRIP

"A Canalside Excursion"

This route offers an easy level walk along the towpath, returning by the same route. It is about 1½ miles from point 17, by Office Lock, to the Armley Mills Industrial Museum, which could be a practical "target" for an afternoon's walk. There are, of course, many other interesting features before (and beyond) the museum. On this page are some of these, all of them linked with the transport theme of this guide.